REFLECTIVE INSIGHTS

Francois Renault

Ideal Publishing
LightPublishing@aol.com
New York, NewYork
United States of America

Second English Edition
F.J. Reynolds©2006

Library of Congress Card Number:
2006927010
International Standard Book Number:
978-0-9621682-3-9

DEDICATION

To every human individual,

for all your earthly sacrifices.

OTHER BOOKS

By Francois Renault

Perfection Is A Process - Book One

Know Your Psyche - Book Two

Your Essence Is Magnetic - Book Three

Balance is Your Foundation - Book Four

Grace Is Your Foundation - Book Five

Picture It Perfect - Book Six

The World is Your Mirror - Book Seven

CONTENTS
Reflective Insights

		page
	Introduction	15
I.	Perfection is a Process	23
II.	Know Your Psyche	39
III.	Your Essence is Magnetic	65
IV.	Balance is your Foundation	79
V.	Grace is your Strength	103
VI.	Picture it Perfect	119
VII.	The World is your Mirror	135
	Bibliography	151

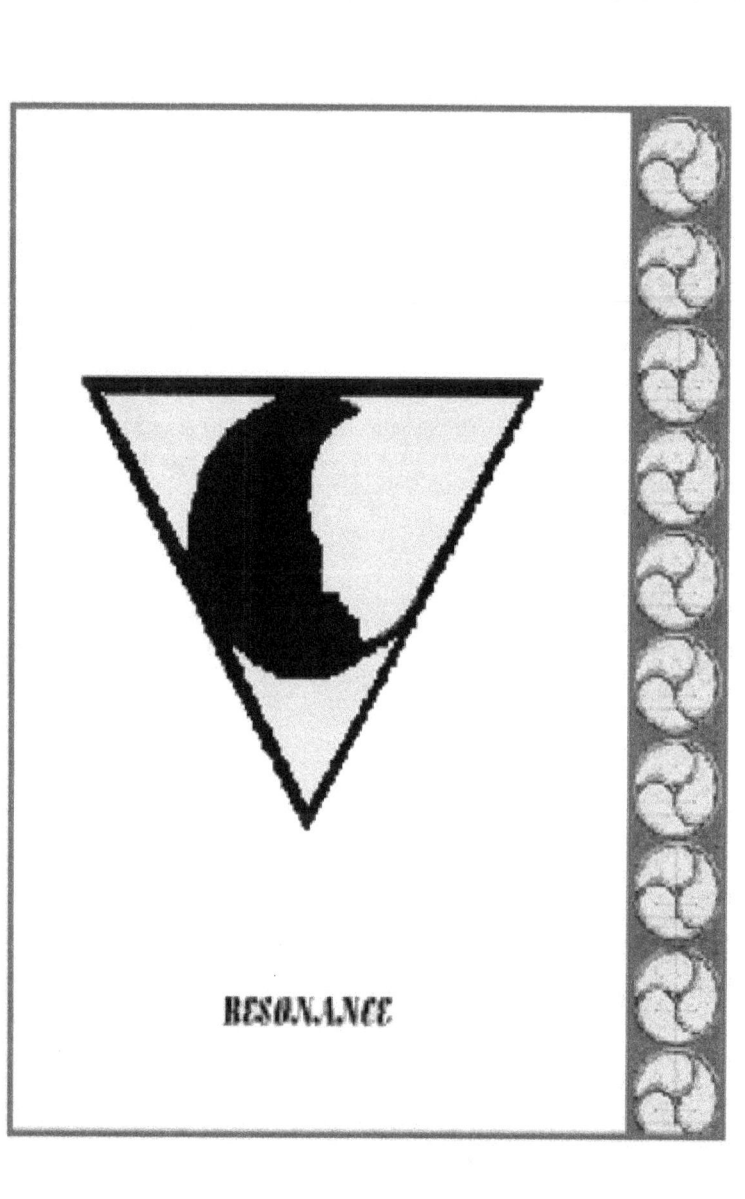

INTRODUCTION

I FEEL, THEREFORE I AM

Welcome to a book that will guide you through your powerful humanity. This book is a synthesis of countless sources of information, including ancient truisms and intuition. An attempt has been made to blend thoughts, ideas, experiences and interpretations into a holistic weave of basic principles that serve as mental conduits into the deepest reaches of the psyche.

Every illustration, chapter title and phrase is meant to trigger archetypal energies that have remained mostly dormant in humanity for millennia. The rest is up to each of us. Even if we are already familiar with some of the topics within these pages, their format and framework have a deeper and more powerful essence than they do independently. Within these pages, concepts are set up as metaphysical formulas that resonate on a deep unconscious level:

The first symbol, seen here in the introduction, has the most powerful meaning: the triangle refers to creativity; the downward direction implies creation within our physical realm; the crescent moon and face refer to the cosmos and humanity as being one and the same.

The main objective of this presentation is to awaken humanity to its creative abilities, which presently lie mostly dormant. But our powers must be coupled with a sense of responsibility or the results can be devastating, as history has proven so many times. Not only are we meant to be custodians of Planet Earth, but we are also to learn how to relate to each other in the highest form possible.

For the most part, the misuse of our abilities has been of the ego's making. Because by itself, it only knows about aggression, control and judgment.

However, humanity does have a Higher Self – a consciousness that derives from the highest dimensional realm. Few individuals are aware of their *"divinity."* And still fewer are willing to admit its existence, because official dogma considers it blasphemous to claim direct connection to the Source of Life. Yet the concept of humans as divine should not frighten either the atheist or the religiously devout. As used here, the term "divinity" does not necessarily refer to a specific god or the Godhead. Rather, *a divine being is simply someone who expresses higher perceptions of understanding and embraces creative powers in a responsible manner.*

That definition is not meant to diminish the brilliance from the concept of divinity; rather, the objective is to ground the notion within our earth-bound egos, which have difficulty with spiritual concepts. To the ego, terms such as Higher Self and divinity seem surreal. Thus a means must be found to align our lower and higher psyches: the ego and Higher Self. Our true consciousness is dualistic, a blending of two natures: we are of the Earth as well as of the cosmos.

Needless to say, humanity has demonstrated its bestial side quite disastrously throughout its existence – so much so, that it seems to have vanquished our creative benevolence. But divinity is equally and rightfully humanity's legacy, whether it is expressed or repressed. Unfortunately, the mere idea of humans as divine beings often causes emotional over-reaction, proving that the ego still has predominance within humanity. Yet the time is quickly arriving when the ego must acknowledge its higher half: the Superconscious. When our lower and higher psyches are finally aligned in full partnership, only then will our potential finally reveal itself.

Discern With The Heart. Regardless of the author's opinions and biases, *Reflective Insights* must stand on its own foundation. Its facts, truisms insights must resonate within your own psyche, or they will simply clutter your mind with more propaganda. So do not believe anything without first discerning its worth within your heart. We must learn to follow our hearts, because the ego is mostly unable to comprehend higher insights.

Unfortunately, people tend to get wrapped up with the messenger rather than the message. Thus it is important to understand that, while everyone can reveal their truth as they perceive it, we all have foibles and battle scars as well. By means of the heart, and through trial and error, we must learn to discern our own truth as best we can; others can only point the way. As we learn about ourselves, we are also learning how to manipulate our reality; the objective is to find our personal success and happiness within the greater reality.

Thus an effort is made to honor inner truth, while also underlining the fact that there is no *one* way to live best. The reality is that we will find personal fulfillment only through self respect and appreciation. This presentation will not make you any more special or extraordinary than you already are. *Instead, the greatest hope is that you will remember your glory as a creature and creator of your reality.*

20

Appreciate your individual understanding of Life, and have the courage to share it with others. No matter how insignificant you may think your life is, your impact and impression on others is extraordinary. Insights are always evolving due to the individual personalities we come in contact with. We will find that those who cross our paths do so for a reason – to exchange views and truths. These people are reality-checks on our own perceptions of truth, since all insights are colored by our experiences.

So question, speculate and dare to dream! But certainly do not get bogged down with petty issues or doubts. As our ego and Divine Self gradually blend in a cosmic dance of perfection, we must keep our minds and hearts open to countless insights that will be flowing our way.

21

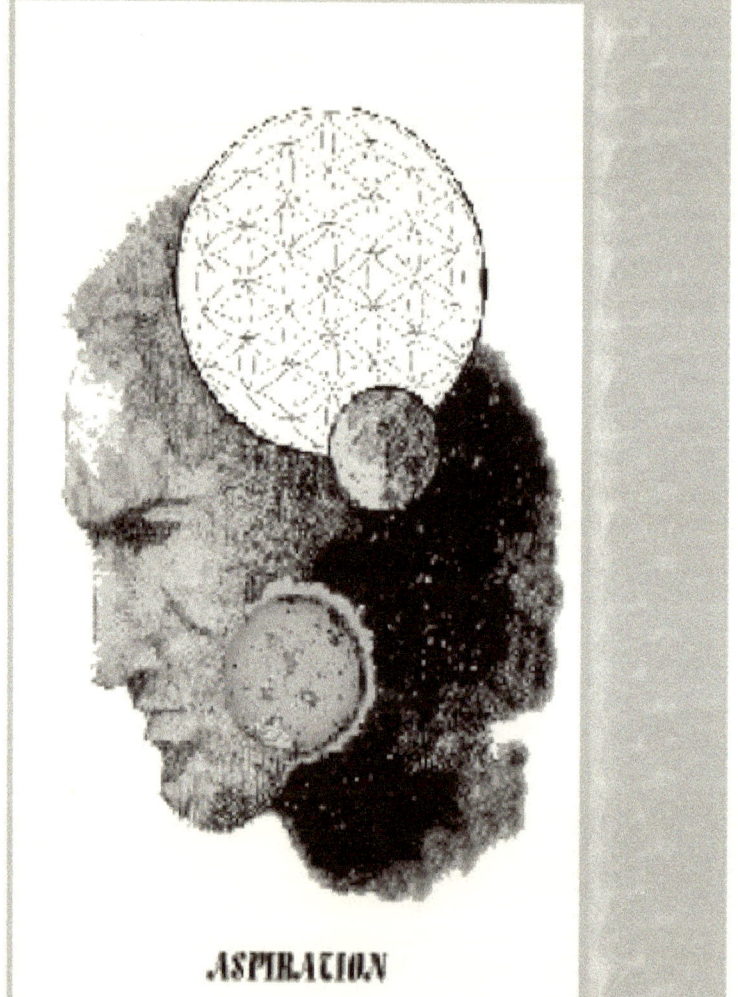

CHAPTER ONE

PERFECTION IS A PROCESS

The most common theme in human nature seems to be the constant search for happiness. This observation may be common sense, yet most of us rarely give it much thought. On the other hand, we often contemplate how to achieve success. Thus the two objectives – happiness and success – are mirror images of each other. While finding happiness seems to be the "illusory" goal in the eternal Game of Life, acquiring a personal sense of accomplishment can be equally frustrating.

Ironically, although the twin goals of happiness and success are the main themes with humanity, most of us are mostly undecided as to what qualifies as their fulfillment. And when we do give it some thought, each of us comes to a different conclusion. Thus it is proposed that *the pursuit of perfection* sums up the main theme of our individual existence. In other words, the pursuit of happiness and success is really about searching for ever greater perfection.

Mostly at an unconscious level, we are all seeking ever greater things – a state of perfection. That seems to be what the Game of Life is all about. Of course, there are cynics who will exclaim that not only is a perfect world unreachable but, if it were, it would be unbearably monotonous. However, their conclusion is erroneous for one reason: there are many degrees to every aspect of Life. Perfection is no exception in this regard. Just as there are degrees of colors, preferences and of all other sorts of things, *there are also many degrees of perfection.* Everything in Life is in degrees; nothing is ever absolute. And when it comes to the ego's development, perfection is a process.

Fear Imprisons. Many individuals are prisoners of their own fears They jail themselves within prisons of their own making. It is unfortunate but true that this is the toughest sentence they will ever serve. Some of their fears are based on insecurities – the fear of being rejected. Other fears are based on the Great Unknown. And still other fears come from a guilty conscience. Yet all of these fears are self-made!

Since Life is self-fulfilling, *we draw into our lives those things and experiences that we desire as well as fear.* We often tell ourselves, "See, I was right to fear that! It happened just the way I feared it would!" And as like attracts like, fear breeds further fear. We create whole experiences of reality based on our own fears. The only way out of this nightmarish prison is to release the dark visions that reside within our minds. *Then we must nurture new insights that promote positive, hopeful qualities.* The only way to do this is to modify our life philosophy: accepting awareness of worst possible scenarios while simultaneously striving for the most ideal one. This approach protects us from the impact that negative expectations can manifest.

Life is About Change. Eventually, many of us

reach a point in our lives when we question our worth. We might ask ourselves, "What have I done to leave a positive mark in the world?" Introspection reflects maturity and a willingness to own up to our responsibilities, for as co-creative souls we do have obligations to Life. The question indicates that we are becoming conscious of our power to direct our own lives. And this awakening is never too late; we can begin our transformation at any time; we can switch gears at this point in our lives. Of course, the sooner we wake up, the more time we have to reach our ideals.

You Are A Pioneer. Life is really an individual experience, for each of us is the center of our own universe, with our own unique outlook and expectations. As a pioneer, you are unrepeatable. No one like you has ever lived before, and there will never be anyone else who is exactly like you.

Therefore, what is most important is that you ascertain for yourself that you are living in the most fulfilling way possible for *you*. You should never accept criticism or advice without feeling that it adds quality to your life. We should play our cards, while letting others play their own. At the same time, we should always keep our mind open to new insights, for they are doorways to ever greater possibilites.

"All humans are created equal" refers to the understanding that all are equally appreciated within the realm of Life. It is the Divine Code – that everyone and everything is respected as divine aspects of Life. Since we are all unique while also being potentially equal, this understanding should discourage us from developing an attitude of either being superior or inferior to anyone. Each person is precious for the uniqueness that he or she expresses. Ultimately, we are all souls empowered with limitless potential. And each of us is given the ability to choose our own fate: we can rise above our present self, if we dare to. But this will happen only if we are willing to accept our divine capabilities.

Although most of us are unaware, our unique energy is vital to the success of the human race. Thus it is important that we learn to appreciate ourselves – we must be true to ourselves! *Each individual consciousness is like a star radiating at its own frequency. Some shine brighter than others only because they choose to enhance their consciousness.*

All individuals are important for their uniqueness. In fact, humanity has thrived on the infinite variety of its members, as each seeks to learn and render service in their own unique way. As a race of people, we are truly a family of kindred souls – spiritual brothers and sisters. Thus we should never feel threatened by the multitude of individualities. On the contrary, our lives are much richer because of them!

We should never believe for one iota that conformity to external values is the only thing that gives us worth. While growing up, we have little choice on this matter, since values are usually instilled within us by adults. Our minds are crammed with values that others insist are the "right" ones. Nor do we have much control over religious beliefs – they are imposed on us as well. However, as adults we have the choice to either automatically live according to our conditioning or to re-evaluate all the instilled values – thereby reclaiming our power. The truth is, our real power is not in pleasing others but in questioning the values we live by. If our only purpose in Life were to please others, not only would we be miserable but humanity would be much poorer because of it.

In the search for ideal expression, it is important to understand that religious dogma is trivial. ***What matters most is the spiritual journey.*** Dogma is for those who resist personal responsibility and wish to have someone to blame for perceived failings. Life consistently demonstrates that there is no *one* way for all to follow, since consciousness desires to express itself in countless ways. Simply put, it is wrong to restrict a soul to one ideology or philosophy. As souls seek experiences, they must be free to express themselves in increasingly broader scopes; they must be free to apply their understanding of Life in the manner they feel most comfortable. We do not have to march to someone else's drumbeat! *We can leave our own footprints!* We are only required to do our best.

Mistakes Are Stepping Stones. Many individuals are afraid to make mistakes in the Game of Life. They would rather fail under values and rules set up by others, than to stand on their own worth. Instead of taking responsibility for their own lives, they blame others – including "God" – for their failures.

But we are inherently obligated to grow every day in every way. We have limitless opportunities to expand our consciousness in every walk of Life, to try things, to possibly fail, to stumble at times and then pick ourselves up again, thereby learning from our "mistakes." *The Divine Rule underscores the understanding that if we are learning from our mistakes, they are simply learning experiences.* In fact, all successes are based on failure. We continue to make "mistakes" only as long as we need to develop an understanding of Life. We should always remember that mistakes are our stepping stones to something greater, for without "negative" and "positive" experiences we would lack the background to create. And how we look at Life makes the difference in how we experience it.

There is no need to fear new insights, for the greatest risk is in not taking chances at all. Success depends on the ability to replace old, unworkable ideas with new progressive ones. In the Bigger Picture, Life is about change – it is certainly not about stagnation or holding onto worn out concepts. Of course, it is important to give ourselves time for contemplation; adopting new thought patterns should be done with deliberation. Everything has its rhythm; everything has its time; and everything has its place in the scheme of things. We are not likely to change overnight, especially after decades of negative conditioning. First we must implant the seeds of new ideas; then we must nurture them with hope and patience. In time, we will be harvesting new possibilities as they sprout within our lives. With every step, every breath and every thought, our lives can change for the better.

Throughout our lives, we often stumble, but we pick ourselves up and continue our journey with courage. There may be times when we think of our lives as unworthy and unimportant; but eventually, we realize that our lives are more important than any problems we face. We realize that we are blessed with the power to overcome the challenges that we are forced to confront. As we go through Life, we continue to expand in consciousness. With every day that passes, we become wiser and more confident in our abilities. We eventually come to realize that *none* of our experiences are wasted, that they are simply stepping stones on the path to perfection.

Sometimes we may run into depressing situations that bring us to a grinding halt. But we eventually learn to work through them because we must. Other times we meet difficult personalities because we must learn to deal with them. Although some experiences seem unbearable, it is precisely during these experiences that we learn the most about living. Life is not about avoiding things but about resolving problems and moving forward. When we are not growing, we are decaying; there is very little stillness in the realm of Life. Thus the choice is to expand or contract in consciousness.

Of course, sometimes we over reach ourselves, and after an inspirational realization may come a depressing negativity. This is why most of us advance in gradual stages, moving through slower cycles. When we overstep ourselves, we have to re-balance ourselves, or we are forced to retrace our steps. *Thus we must grow at our own rate, by our own terms, in our own manner, by way of our own unique self.* Indeed, enlightenment is an individual matter!

Greatness In The Making. The purpose of human existence is to move towards perfection, to ever higher levels of expression. In simpler terms, the purpose of Life is to live a life of purpose. Life is its own question as well as its own answer! While it is true that our egos are of an animal nature, often causing us to behave insanely, it is equally true that we are blessed with divinity. More than any other creature, we have a responsibility as co-creators with Life, for we are animals embodying divinity. Spiritual expression is the goal as well the essence of our existence. Because of our divine inheritance, we are required to learn how to apply and control our consciousness. And as we do, we are learning to manipulate universal energy in a creative fashion.

The word "Life" is capitalized to emphasize the Divine Consciousness instilled within all things. In other words, Life is awareness; and awareness is Life. However, no religious representation is made regarding the sanctity of Life; religious dogma has no place within these pages, because practical living is the only objective.

The sanctity of Life is everywhere, in everything, inside each and every one of us. We are channels through which Life expresses Itself. Even the rhythms of Nature manifest expressions of Life. There is an elementary consciousness within all things, alive or otherwise. For all things are simply a composite of pulsating frequencies. *At the subatomic level, everything is energy, and energy is everything.* In other words, Life expresses Itself according to universal laws of energy. It is simply basic physics.

Focus On The Moment. Because it thinks in extremes, the ego often has difficulty accepting the intelligent nature of Life. Our polarized thinking of right/wrong, God/Creation, us/them often creates friction with the deepest reality of Life. When we approach Life with a narrow mind, we fail to perceive the oneness of Life, and we erroneously convince ourselves that there is nothing beyond the material world.

Thus, until we are prepared to embrace the sanctity of all Life, we should focus on what we *can* comprehend at the moment. Taking one step at a time, it is best not to force ourselves to accept or reject concepts we are unable to understand at the moment. We learn what we can, when we can, in the manner that we can – for our worth is in respecting

36

ourselves exactly as we are.

37

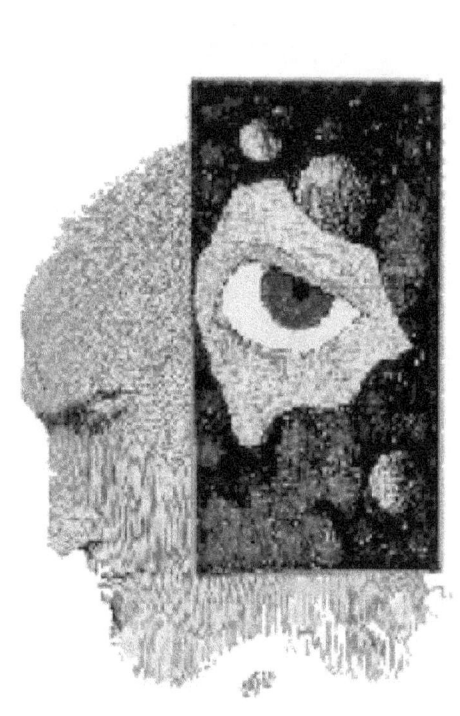

CONSCIOUSNESS

CHAPTER TWO

KNOW YOUR PSYCHE

One of the most unique things about humanity is its quality of intelligence. Being of such importance, one would expect that there would be a standardized definition of intelligence universally accepted. Yet it seems difficult for researchers to agree on a uniform definition – perhaps because human intelligence is quite unique. The study and measurement of intelligence has been an important research topic for over 100 years, with researchers still unable to agree on a common understanding. Thus the challenge is to first understand the nature of human intelligence and then to define its qualities.

The Human Equation. There is an ancient directive that was inscribed over the doorways to temples: "*Man, Know Thyself!*" This decree inspired many individuals to perfect themselves. Whoever first wrote these immortal words was highly insightful, realizing that the attainment of wisdom, balance and happiness come only as we understand ourselves. Without a doubt, it is important to understand every aspect of ourselves: *who, what, how and why:*

• *Who*: Most prominently, we have the ego to contend with, for it is the most basic essence of our psychological makeup. The ego, which is the lower self or undersoul, is the "who" of our physical presence and is derived from our base animal instincts. It is both our strength as well as our Achilles' heal. On the one hand, our ego grounds us in reality by discerning all information that comes to us, always attempting to maintain some sense of order. Yet the ego will also deny and distort truth at all costs, if it finds it threatening to its simplistic sense of order – no matter how strong the logic may be. In fact, everyone holds contradictory views, because the ego is never able to completely consolidate all the facts into a coherent reality.

Being of a simple nature, the human ego is driven by two needs: to be rewarded as well as to avoid punishment. Thus it is motivated to maintain a sense of security by replicating what it considers successful. Its need for self-preservation often manifests as a struggle of its animal instincts versus our divine nature. Socially constructive acts are possible only because the ego has what are described as "movable boundaries." This refers to its ability to expand its definition of self to include the welfare of others. Examples include parents caring for their offspring, friends looking after each other, athletes playing as a team, and comrades demonstrating loyalty to each other. Obviously, the ego is not always completely of a selfish nature, since it does have the capacity to include others within its sphere of concern.

As a means of insuring survival, the ego often relies on fear. This is why so many individuals live their lives within the realm of constant fear – because their personality is mostly based on their ego. Their every decision is based on avoiding negative repercussions; every decision is defined by fear. Although it is true that some fears make self-preservation possible, it must be understood that constructive fears are based on logic, while many other fears are irrational. Destructive forms of fear tend to lead to vicious circles of self-fulfilling prophecies.

When we base our lives on irrational fears, we energize them, thereby attracting more of the very things we fear. Then when they become our reality, it reinforces the belief that we are smart to live by means of those fears. Thus we must discriminate intelligently, releasing illogical fears that impede our development. Such types of fear only force us to contract further into control dramas.

As with fear, the expression of emotion can also be excessive, although it is normally desirable when expressed properly. We must discriminate our emotions in an intelligent manner. However, feeling guilty about expressing anger or sadness, for example, can lead to a destructive undercurrent. Similarly to the way steam pressure builds within in a kettle, emotional energy can also develop destructive force, eventually requiring an outlet. If the emotional pressure takes a long time to build, the consequences can be explosive.

- *What*: It is also important to understand what we are: *non-physical entities residing in physical bodies*. While we utilize brains of an electro-magnetic nature, our corporal vehicles bestow us with the ability to relocate ourselves in the world. We should not under appreciate our brains and bodies, for they allow the soul to pursue awesome adventures in Life.

Understanding the "what" of our physical expression helps us understand many of our troubling disorders. For example, some mental problems resonate from an unbalanced electro-magnetic system, which are similar to bio-electric short circuits. Once ingrained within the electro-magnetic complex, the short circuits can be difficult to correct. Since such disorder reverberates throughout the mental and bodily structures, the problem must be treated in a holistic manner.

Research has made tremendous progress in regards to understanding the basis of many imbalances within the body. Pioneers continue to pursue research into the bio-magnetic causes of many of our problems, making steady inroads into understanding how it intricately affects our mental and physical health.

• *How*: Although our brains and bodies are obviously of a biological nature, as research deepens, we will come to perceive their electro-magnetic quality as well. Medical science has unequivocally demonstrated that:

1) nerve and immune systems are interconnected; and
2) that the body's systems communicate with each other via electro-magnetic signals. This bio-electrical communication is accomplished both directly through the nervous system as well as indirectly by hormonal impulses. Thus a wide collection of devices have been invented to measure the bio-electric nature of the body and brain.

- *Why*: The "why" of human existence is unquestionably the most difficult for humanity to concede. Religions, sciences and politics have all taken turns at making sense of the human presence. The bottom line is that, born with a superior consciousness, humanity has always been accomplishing what it was born to do: creating, learning and improving. As a parent will often observe, children can create much havoc while maturing into adulthood. Only after reaching adulthood do most individuals manifest their skills for the benefit of society.

Historically, the same holds true for humanity. As a young species, we have hated and destroyed in the name of a God which, ironically, we declare all merciful and loving. The savagery that continues today in the world need not be related here, as it is already overexposed by the media.

Unfortunately, there is little sensationalism in the quiet presence of enlightened individuals. Thus spiritual goodness rarely makes it to the front line of the media. Therefore, the individual who wishes to pursue his divine worth cannot depend on public approval – it simply is not newsworthy! Without fanfare, enlightened souls must quietly accept their responsibility as a *co-creator with Life*. Coming to terms as co-creators is a lifelong project of ever growing consciousness. Motives, desires and views have to be constantly scrutinized, for all things eventually become distorted, and corruption seems to be a common thread in all things human.

The Multi-Dimensional Mind. Throughout the evolution of humanity, its most valuable asset has been its mind. It should be understood that the mind is without physical tangibility – in other words, we should not confuse the mind with the brain, as happens frequently. The two are completely separate faculties: *while the mind is our true consciousness, it uses the brain to express its will.*

Intuitive awareness is one of our "spiritual" expressions. It has been theorized to be the Oversoul's communications to the ego, the undersoul. Often expressed as inspiration, it can be defined as "knowing without rationalization." This inner knowing can be of invaluable assistance when issues are not easily defined by logic or reasoning.

Another type of spiritual knowing is *telepathy*. Although most of us do not consider ourselves telepathic, nevertheless we all experience it on occasion. Sometimes we are able to inadvertently pick up telepathic messages because they are either imbued with a powerful feeling or are sent with a sense of urgency. Other times, the Conscious Mind happens to be in a receptive state at the right moment. Telepathic messages are always sent and received as symbols. And if they are infused with emotional energy, they tend to express stronger signals.

Mainstream individuals can have telepathic exchanges, although they are usually unaware of the ongoing process. For example, most of us have experienced the odd feeling of being stared at. When looking up, we might lock eyes with the person staring at us. Although it may feel surreal, this type of experience is more than mere coincidence: it validates the existence of unseen energy exchanges between humans.

The Subconscious Mind operates with symbolic representations; it hears, reads, speaks and senses all communication via meaningful symbols. Clairvoyants, for example, receive their prophetic visions in symbolic form. Their Conscious Minds must then decipher the symbolic representations for their meaning. Thus predictions can be faulty when their symbolism is misinterpreted.

What is described here is only a simplification of theoretical psychic abilities. Most important is the *essence* of the message: That we are much more than simply the "walking wounded"; we carry the potential for real, psychic senses. These senses are a manifestation of our real selves, so if the reader is inspired to pursue further research, then the intention will have been accomplished. People must become aware of their potential; they must understand that there is much more to them than has been obvious. The bottom line is that we are more than our bodies. *We are our minds,* which are not simply by-products of the brain; and our bodies are not mannequins from which spring our consciousness. Rather, our real identity inhabits and manipulates the body.

Although the human mind is really one essence, it can be subdivided into three parts, in order to better understand its many attributes. The three minds are labeled as the: (1) Conscious, (2) Subconscious and (3) Superconscious. Working in unison, each mind has its distinctive set of abilities. To best understand the complexity of our triad mind, we can apply the analogy of an iceberg:

> *Imagine a large iceberg in the ocean. The Conscious and Subconscious Minds are akin to the iceberg, but the vastness of the ocean represents the power of the Superconscious! In contrast, the Conscious Mind (ego) only constitutes the tip of the iceberg; while the portion under water compares to the*

Subconscious. And just as the vastness of the ocean implies great depth and energy, so are the resources that are available to the Superconscious Mind.

• *Conscious Mind.* This mind is neither the most important or least of the three. It is the first to be described only because it dominates our interactions within 3D reality. The ego (undersoul) relies on the Conscious Mind, utilizing it to direct its will in the world and to deal with mundane matters. Its nature requires that it organize and analyze the world by polarizing it into extremes and contrasts. This manner of perception portrays Life in simplistic dichotomies of logical and illogical, good and bad, right and wrong, male and female, etc. It selectively filters and simplifies information in this manner because that is the only system it is aware of.

By accepting only input compatible with its expectations, values and needs, the ego/Conscious Mind is able to manage the constant bombardment of bewildering data – even if not in the clearest manner.

Its main purpose is to focus, organize and simplify our perception of the world. Otherwise, the amount of incoming information would overwhelm us and thus prevent us from steering through the world.

For normal day to day affairs, this form of processing is normally sufficient. Unfortunately, it is locked into a very narrow view of reality. And it finds it difficult to change its angle on Life, to understand spiritual insights. Nevertheless, it is still possible for it to embrace higher principles, by taking a leap of faith. Because the ego decides what feelings are permitted into its consciousnes, *it can choose to embrace spiritual insights through feeling*. It learns that specific feelings are related to specific understandings. For example, it can understand the concept of grace by relating it to unconditional love.

- *Subconscious Mind.* While the Conscious Mind is described as the commanding one, the Subconscious has attributes of a servant mentality. It is like the portion of iceberg floating beneath the surface of water, having vast potential for powerful transformations.

As long as our consciousness remains in positive mode, constructive patterns are imprinted within the servant mind. But since it is incapable of rationalizing, it only knows to submit to any and all mental patterns, without discrimination. Its role is simply to record. Because the ego controls access to the Subconscious, it decides what is recorded. Thus it is extremely important that we be fully conscious of our thoughts and feelings at all times, for the planting of feelings and ideas today dictate our view of Life in the future.

Being computer-like, the Subconscious functions much like the auto-pilot on an aircraft. Because it is extremely impressionable, mirroring our thoughts and feelings, it readily stores our personality traits. Through the years, it records our habits, attitudes, prejudices, philosophies and memories. In fact, it remembers _everything_! And it holds our self image as well – regardless of whether it is good or bad. It doesn't discriminate; it doesn't rationalize; and it doesn't make judgements. It simply records. Although a poor master, it is an excellent servant. When given suggestions of any kind, it performs marvelously, following all directions accordingly. Most efficiently recorded are strong, repetitive affirmations – especially if they are imbued with strong feeling.

- *Superconscious Mind.* This is our highest mind, an expression of our Oversoul. While the Submind is simply a receptacle for information, *the Supermind is our direct connection to the vast primordial essence found throughout the universe.* This essence can be likened to an ocean of pure energy and is often referred to as the Universal Mind.

The Supermind is our connection to Life; it offers us infinite resources that are always at our disposal. Through the ages, many mystics have been aware of its existence and realized its amazing potential – because accessing it can lead to miraculous experiences.

But there is so much more to our Higher Mind! Through it, we can understand concepts the Conscious Mind can only begin to contemplate. The Universal Mind speaks to us via the Supermind, since they are directly connected and are of the same essence. It is our conduit to intuition, insights and inspirations – communications from the Source of Life. The term "psychic" communication is an appropriate term for these, since the word is originally derived from the Greek word for "soul."

Possibly, the one exception to its powers is its inability to place judgement on anyone or anything; its nature is somewhat similar to the Subconscious in this respect. It only knows to express grace on all things, for it perceives everything to be connected and of divine origin. However, it does have the capacity to guide us, advise us and direct us according to its higher perception of reality.

The Dualistic Brain. Just as we have a triad mind – a consciousness of three minds – we have two brains or hemispheres. And likewise, they work together in a complementary manner.

It is important to our success that we understand that our brain is NOT our mind. Too frequently, this distinction is left unclarified by academics. Often, they are the number one culprit in confusing the two terms, using "brain" and "mind" synonymously, as if they had the same characteristics and functions. Rather, the truth is that we are our minds; and our minds utilize the brain to express themselves in the 3D world. If many researchers refuse to believe in the spiritual realm, rejecting the concept of a human soul, it is partially because controlling forces make every effort to prevent its validation. For if the soul's existence were declared a reality, it would open up a "can of worms" – a Pandora's box of sorts. Except that the forthcoming influences would not be evil but enlightenment! These "controlling forces" have their insidious reasons for undermining knowledge of our true nature. Suffice to say that it is certainly not for our benefit but to keep the upper hand.

The ego/Conscious Mind uses the brain to express itself in Life, thereby manifesting its will in 3D reality. The brain simply functions as a type of control panel, while the ego is the true source of our willpower. And although the ego acts as our undersoul in the physical world, it is only a by-product of the Conscious Mind.

The brain itself is divided into two halves, known as the left and right hemispheres. While each portion can process entirely different types of thinking, they can overlap as well. Since they are connected, the two brains tend to work together, sharing information through the corpus callosum. In this presentation, the brain is only described in generalizations because the objective is simply to emphasize the distinction between brain and mind.

• *The Left Hemisphere.* The left side of the brain controls mostly the right side of the body. It tends to handle those thought patterns dealing with linear, quantitative processes, such as mathematics, measurement of time and space, logic, deduction, rationalization and analytical thought. It is more dominant with calculations, math and logical abilities. Generally speaking, the left brain prefers parts (to the whole) – such as functions, symbols, instructions, structure and specifics in general.

• *The Right Hemisphere.* The right side of the brain controls mostly the left side of the body. It focuses on comprehensive, qualitative thinking, which can include creativity, pattern recognition, symmetry, comparisons, imagination, artistic appreciation, feeling, intuition and abstract thought. It is more dominant with spatial abilities, such as face recognition, visual imagery and music. Generally speaking, the right brain prefers the whole (to parts) – such as appearances, pictures, spontaneity and the "bigger picture."

Clearly, the ideal is to develop a type of balanced thinking. When we utilize all of our cognitive skills in perfect harmony, the results can be exponential. For example, the blending of logic and intuition leads to perspectives that result in more successful performances.

Although there are many aspects of the brain worthy of understanding, covering all of them is beyond the scope of this book. However, one aspect is definitely important enough to discuss – the pineal gland, for it is an integral part of our spiritual equation:

Pineal, Lightning Rod. Although it is not technically a part of the brain, this gland has a strategic closeness to emotional centers in the brain; it is also directly connected to the spinal cord. Its prime location bestows it the potential of functioning as an electro-magnetic lightning rod – a gateway to different states of mind. Sounds, electro-magnetic frequencies, hormonal secretions and even thoughts all have the capacity to activate its capabilities, causing it to vibrate as an antenna. As a doorway, it can give us access to an amazing variety of other-dimensional worlds.

Shaped like a pine cone, its size varies from that of a grain of rice to that of a pea. Located in the center of the brain, it lies behind and above the pituitary gland, which is a little behind the root of the nose. It has a strategic attachment to the third ventricle as well, which is filled with cerebrospinal fluid. Unlike other parts of the brain which come in pairs, the pineal gland is singular without a comparable part. Furthermore, its location in the center of the brain, as well as its presence in many other species, suggests that it is a much older part of our brain system.

Within most animals, the pineal seems to function simply as a type of light receptor or monitor. It helps regulate hibernation, metabolism and seasonal breeding. While in humans its major effects appear to be rhythmic in nature, affecting sleep patterns and dream states. Before the onset of puberty, it begins to shrink; and by the age of 12, it begins to calcify. By adulthood it is mostly hardened, atrophied and dormant – probably from lack of use. It is possible that environmental factors may also play a role in its impairment. For example, research has revealed that fluoride may accumulate in the pineal gland, thereby speeding its calcification. Fortunately, those who appreciate the pineal's psychic implications have studied ways to revitalize and reinstate its potential.

Its anatomy is derived from specialized cells that originate at the roof of the mouth. Interestingly, it is *not* made up of brain tissue, as might be expected. Rather, studies have found that the pineal gland contains light-sensitive cells similar to those in the eye's retina. In fact, its structure in more primitive animals can be quite startling. Its manifestation as an eye-like structure in various lower vertebrates testifies to its function as a type of "seeing" apparatus. It actually manifests as an eye in some species, possessing a lens, cornea and retina like a normal eye. However, as a third eye, it develops as a mirror image of a regular eye, rendering it incapable of processing *regular* vision.

Theoretically, the purpose of the pineal in

humans is for the perception of psychic "vision." Although this theory can be controversial and provocative to cynics, it has never been proven otherwise. Considering its amazingly eye-like structure in some animals, skeptics are challenged to disprove its function as a psychic apparatus. The very idea of a "third eye" has long fascinated ordinary people and mystics alike throughout the world. Especially in ancient times, various cultures even practiced drilling a tiny hole in the center of the forehead, purportedly to stimulate the third eye. This procedure was a highly refined surgical procedure, performed only by the best highly skilled specialists.

The pineal gland has a purpose beyond what contemporary science understands; its potential is much grander than is presently comprehensible to conservative researchers. However, as humanity's spiritual evolution progresses, the pineal will become central to empirical research. While its magnificence is only suspected by some, its secrets will eventually be revealed when the time is right.

For now, we can contemplate the miraculous possibilities that will be forthcoming in the near future. Of all the adventures taken by humanity, those into spiritual and dimensional spheres will be the most rewarding yet. We need only maintain an open mind and an open heart, while appreciating the new avenues and perceptions that will be manifesting soon.

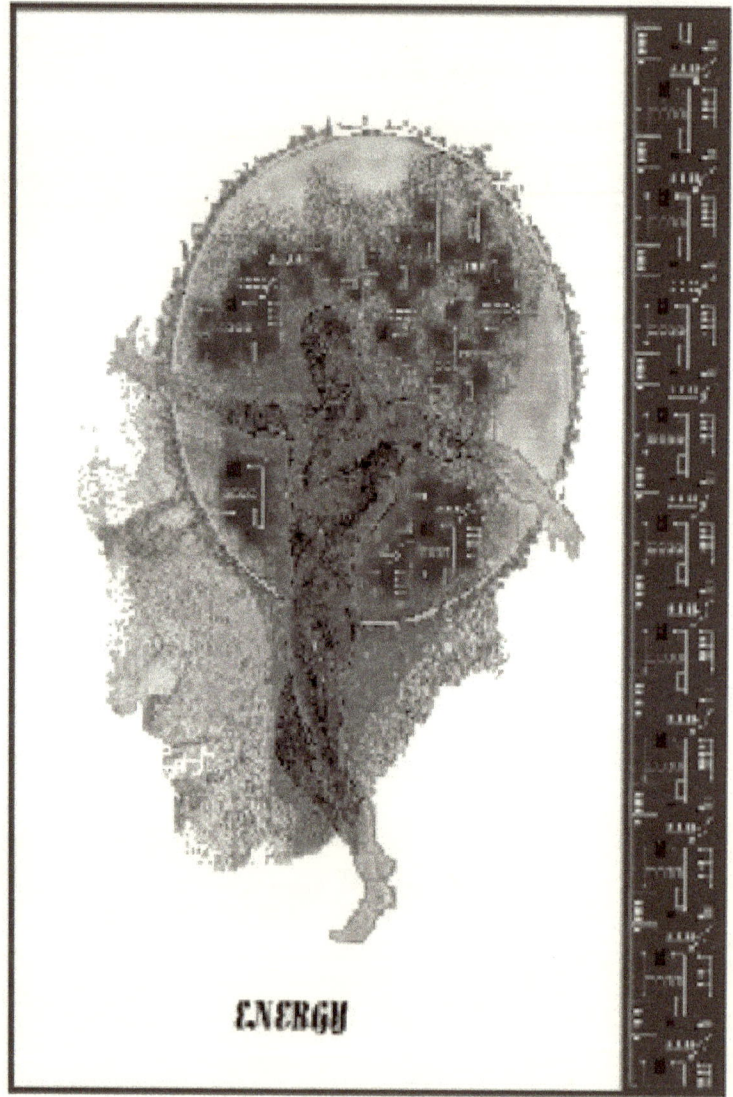

CHAPTER THREE

YOUR ESSENCE IS MAGNETIC

Many insightful researchers have long suspected that the key to understanding the universe may lie within the workings of the human body. Because the more we learn about how our bodies function, the more we come to appreciate what marvelous creations they are. We are slowly realizing that our bodies are a reflection of the cosmos, with the same principles of physics inherent within them as are apparently active throughout the universe.

It is elementary knowledge that the body requires chemical sustenance to maintain itself in a healthy, balanced state. What is not well understood by mainstream society is that the body also requires nourishment via electro-magneticism (EM). This is because its cells are simultaneously matter and electro-magnetic in nature. While the body generates minute magnetic fields, these magnetic fields interact with, and are affected by, external magnetic forces as well.

The Fundamental Matrix. Almost certainly, electro-magnetism exists throughout the universe as a fundamental factor – a major energy force responsible for the ordering of all things. In fact, electro-magnetism may be the dominant principle that regulates three-dimensional reality.

Few are aware that the Earth is in fact a giant magnet, generating its own invisible force field. It emanates like a great, all-pervading ghost power, influencing everything within its sphere – and actually reaching into the vast stretches of outer space. Even as we read these words, the Earth's magnetic field is passing through and affecting our bodies in ways we still do not understand fully.

An intellectual genius once wrote: "The magnet is the king of all secrets." And indeed it is! For without magnetism, Life would not exist on Earth in its present form. As commonplace as it is, we have only begun to decipher the basic nature of electromagnetism. Its most powerful secrets still lie deep within the mystery of Life itself.

What we do know about magnetism is very limited and simple; but it is fundamental to further research:
- *Without it, the higher forms of life would cease to exist on Earth. Experiments on animals kept in metal cages that shield them from the Earth's magnetism demonstrate dire results. Within a few weeks of being insulated from magnetism, their bodies progressively deteriorate and eventually die.*
- *The force field created by a magnet is not uniform in strength. It is strongest at its poles and weakest at its center. The Earth's field is no different. A compass needle will dip less when it is at the equator than it would at either pole.*
- *Electricity & magnetism are complementary forces; they are related, as if reflections of*

one another. Neither force seems capable of existing exclusively of the other; they are simply variations of each other. We know this to be fact, because an electric current passing through a wire sets up a magnetic field around that wire, and magnetism can be used to generate an electric current.

The Human Matrix. The complexity of energy movement within our bodies surpasses present understanding of electro-magnetism. But we do grasp a basic understanding of the principles involved. For example, it has been established that our health is affected by the availability of external magnetic fields. Under normal circumstances the body interacts with – and apparently absorbs something from – the planet's magnetic field. This constant exchange of energy between the body and the electro-magnetic environment is important for maintaining its bio-chemical balance. However, sometimes the body's electro-magnetic equilibrium is thrown out of sync. Without proper metabolic equilibrium, the body is then unable to fulfill its energy needs in an efficient manner.

Within the body are located what are called "energy vortices," radiating outwards as spirals of electro-magnetic waves. Besides energy vortices, the body also radiates energy through skeletal and nerve structures as well. In fact, many biological avenues serve as conduits for energy transference. The major vortices connect with countless minor ones as well; which in turn correlate with organ and gland counterparts. Every body part is nourished by radiating energy. When the energy vortices increasingly grow dormant due to aging or illness, the recipient organs and glands suffer as a consequence. Thus it is important to keep the vortices stimulated, encouraging them to remain open and expressive so that they can express the body's energy flow.

There are numerous theories that attempt to explain the aging process. But research continues searching for one unifying hypothesis. What is needed is one theory disclosing the aging process in a comprehensive manner. Undoubtedly, many influences will be found to contribute to the aging process – with electro-magnetism probably being the central factor.

Scientists do generally accept two basic lines of thought on the aging process. One is that it is primarily predetermined by genetic programing. Secondly is that it is affected by environmental factors as well. Of course, both views are equally valid to various degrees. For instance, research has determined that cells are definitely limited in the number of times they can divide. The only cells which divide indefinitely in test tube cultures are cancerous ones. Also, it has been determined that certain chemical substances can increase the number of healthy cell replications.

Pioneering scientists have theorized that our DNA strands have electro-magnetic counterparts as well These theoretical magnetic codes are wrapped around the biological ones, with the two systems maintaining continuous correspondence with each other. Together, the two code systems express themselves as an *energy matrix*, which is the blueprint that guides the developmental process of specific bodily attributes. In other words, the codes (as a matrix) create and maintain the body according to genetic instruction.

In accordance with this theory, aging is due to corruption of the body's matrix. As the genetic force field accumulates defects, it loses it ability to sustain the body's vortices. Since the body cannot function properly without a clear set of instructions, its vitality withers away and eventually results in death.

The Fountain Of Life. There have been many legends and fables regarding the eternal quest for a "Fountain of Youth." This involves a special type of water that intercepts the aging process and restores youth. It is now suspected that such a "fountain" may eventually be created through technology. It would flow not with water but with the forces of Life – water simply being symbolic for vital energies. Nourishing the genetic matrix with this *"Fountain of Life"* would revitalize the body's energy flow, bringing it back to a youthful state.

Although an actual "Fountain of Life" has not yet been constructed, there is still much we can do to promote physical vitality. For example, simple magnetic therapy can be applied to reinforce the body's EM matrix. Basic magnetism will not correct all aging problems but it can minimize many of the related issues – possibly increasing life spans. As understanding and technology improve, so will our capacity to recalibrate and enhance the body's energy systems. The result will be an increasingly greater quality and duration of human life.

Indeed, with improved tools, we will become wondrous engineers of the human body. Already, we affect and modify our own bodies according to our attitudes. That is, through the power of our thoughts, we mold our bodies into something strong or decrepit, into something beautiful or ugly. Technology will simply amplify that control, so that we will be able to increase our life spans many times over.

Energy Devices. According to ancient documents, the practice of magnet therapy was developed thousands of years ago. Records show that ancient cultures had a basic understanding of electro-magnetic effects and of its importance as a healing mechanism. Several writings mention magnetic ores as having a force field akin to the fundamental life force.

Modern science has been catching up with the ancient practice of magnetic therapy, having re-discovered basic premises. For example, it has been established that electro-magnetic currents definitely support metabolic functions, such as formation of amino acids within the cells. When a magnet is applied to the body, the external magnetic force field induces electrical currents, thereby jump starting EM flow within cells. If used properly, electro-magnetic therapy can be applied safely in a self-care program. (Of course, serious health issues should always be referred to professionals.) The only potential risk is in over saturation with magnetic energy. Although it has not been clear what this "saturation" entails, the effect is real; but the specifics of the cause are not fully understood. With over saturation, the body perceives the effect as a threat, because it can interfere with the cells' own electro-magnetic resonance.

Modern EM medical devices range from very tiny, simple magnets to large machines capable of generating high magnitudes of field strength. For example, electric currents are sometimes applied to encourage the regrowth of bone and nerve tissue. Other devices are useful for restarting the heart. Still other devices are used to measure brain waves. And so on. New types of magnetic devices are being invented every year, for various applications. Thus, by means of electro-magnetism, scientists are not only able to direct the body to heal, but they are also able read the body's energy requirements.

Any magnetic field will penetrate the body, affecting the functioning of nerves, organs, glands and cells. For instance, a basic magnetic field will stimulate metabolism and increase the amount of oxygen available to cells. Oxygenation can function similarly to antibiotics by destroying bacterial, fungal and viral infections. It is theorized that a magnetic field passing through the body causes negatively charged DNA to draw oxygen out of the bloodstream and into the cells. This type of therapy may also help normalize metabolic problems that cause conditions such as cellular edema and acidosis.

New Angles. We have only begun uncovering the basic principles of magnetic therapy. New perspectives and applications will include studying specific effects from combining various elements with magnetic fields. Because individual factors can affect the frequency of a magnetic field, these factors can be modulated to create unique health benefits. The adjustments may include the type of magnetized material, the strength of the field, as well as the shape of the magnet – among many other variables. Undoubtedly, research on the magnetization of different substances – such as minerals and plastics – will lead to new astounding discoveries within this field. Such endeavors will not only help us envision new healing devices, but they will also lead to deeper

76

insights on the workings of the life force.

77

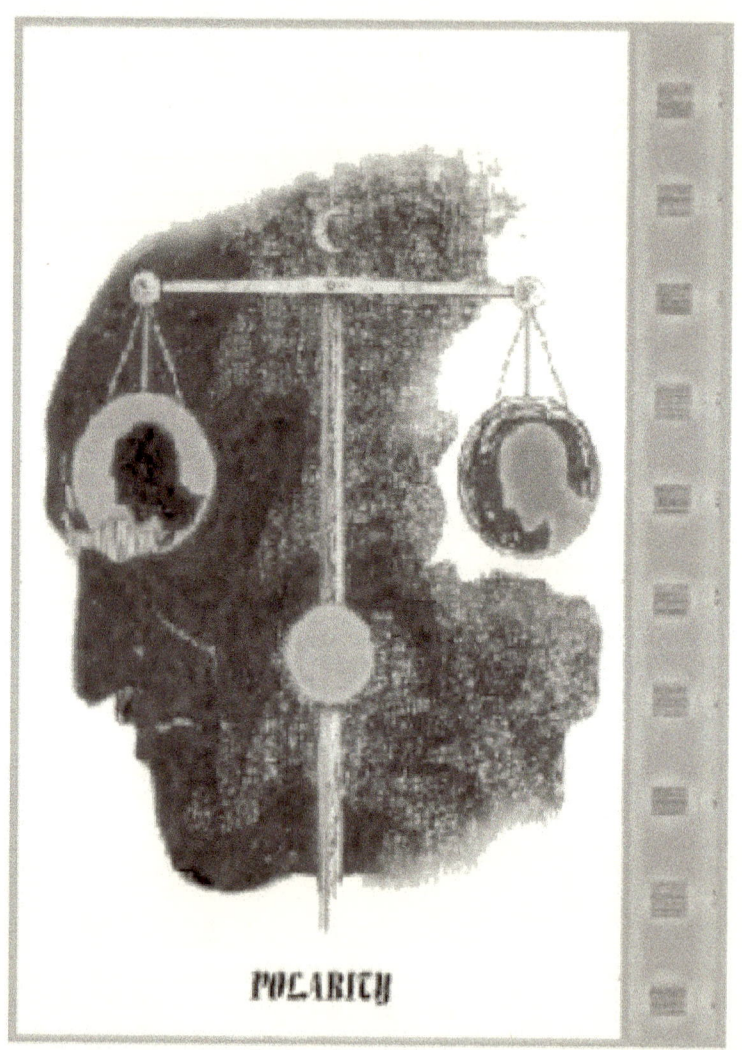

CHAPTER FOUR

BALANCE IS YOUR FOUNDATION

The struggle of inflexion versus balance creates a constant tension of pushing and pulling throughout reality, an interplay of polarizing forces. However, this fluctuation always leads back to a state of balance, for this is also the natural state of the universe. Otherwise, it would quickly collapse with chaos. While everything in Life interacts in perpetual play and counter-play, the *Dance of Equilibrium* moves eternally to maintain stability.

Without the Principle of Polarity, Life could not exist an orderly, living expression. For one thing, there would be no movement, no growth and no change. Sometimes this principle is quite obvious; but most often it is subtle and not easily perceived. As it is with the totality of Life, polarity is equally pertinent to human beings. Our minds and bodies are subject to universal principles as well.

The Tao Principle. At the most basic level, the eternal dynamics of polarity is described as a struggle of opposing forces, as represented by the *Tao*. This is an ancient symbol which depicts the two creative forces of *yin* and *yang* – the seeds of receptivity and proactivity, female and male or darkness and light – which blend and integrate with each other, thereby creating Life. Polarizing forces take many forms, with a wide variation; they are simply expressions of opposites. This is the basis of all things in the universe, regardless of whether they are labeled "good" or "bad." Essentially, it is *not* a matter of "evil" versus "good" – although this can certainly be one of its many multi-faceted aspects.

By understanding this most basic principle of Life, it becomes one of our greatest teachers. It is only because we are able to compare and contrast opposites that we are able to develop an

understanding of Life, because:
- *Without opposites we cannot have comparisons and contrasts;*
- *Without comparisons and contrasts we cannot have knowledge;*
- *Without knowledge we cannot grow in understanding.*

While we should acknowledge and understand the all-encompassing nature of the Polarity Principle, it is equally important to not become obsessed with it. For example, when we over-emphasize a strong belief in "goodness" and "badness" it throws our perception of Life out of balance. This happens because an emphasis on the "good" and "bad" can leads us to focus on the "bad" in everything. On the other hand, a healthy awareness of the Tao Principle helps us maintain a balanced perspective of all things, including an understanding of evil and its role within the bigger picture. Thus, as we strive to attain ever higher and wider states of consciousness, it becomes even more important that we master polarity.

It is a fact that there are cycles of ups and downs in different scenarios of Life. This is equally true with our personal lives. And when we are in "down" mode, it is especially tempting to linger on the negative aspects of things. Sometimes, not only do we tend to focus on our own flaws but also on what we perceive to be flaws in other people and things. Therefore, as we move through lower cycles, we should make an extra effort to strive for balance. As we master the lesson of balance, our view of Life will become less distorted, and it will support us from falling into even lower levels of expression. If we wish to maximize our potential, then we must learn how to balance all aspects of our lives.

Forces Of Dissonance. Everyone experiences cycles of low expression throughout their lives. And when we fall out of balance, we sometimes turn to living by our wits, defaulting to our ego's abilities.. These are times when we focus on our egos, because we lose our connection with the source of our intuition: our Higher Selves. But the ego only knows to depend on sheer willpower to shove its way through the world. But when we stumble our way through Life in this manner, we exacerbate the situation because we develop even more imbalances in our lives – in body, mind and spirit. It is ignorance that compels us to solely depend on our egos, for when the ego is aligned with its Higher Self, we tend to surf on the waves of Life. Otherwise, there is fear and a sense of struggle, as we feel overwhelmed by the sea of Life.

Eventually and gradually, through trial and error, most of us develop our own sense of equilibrium. When we tire of living in survival mode and realize that we wish to move to higher levels of expression, we become aware of inspirational standards by which to live. The Principle of Polarity is part of this understanding – that everything has its place in the scheme of things. It encourages us to perceive the beauty and necessity for everything, that all things and experiences have their place and importance. As our consciousness evolves, we grow to realize that the "negative" things give the "positive" things their significance. Without ugliness, beautiful things would not be appreciated; without badness, goodness would not be recognized. And so ultimately, everything has its importance in Life.

States of imbalance can also be understood in the context of social psychology. Many psychologists have demonstrated that the average human being is motivated predominantly by insecurities. And to compensate for their fears, they strive to control the things, situations and people around them. This is usually an unconscious reaction.

Efforts at psychological domination take place in every aspect and level of social interaction: from the family level to the global arena. Everywhere, human interactions are a sea of energy competition. And in order to maintain an equilibrium of energy and keep from drowning, people manipulate each other in countless ways.

When two individuals find themselves in a common, competitive environment, one will often attempt to take a more dominant role. But this scenario can have negative consequences. Not only can efforts at domination throw a relationship off balance but it can also create a sense of anxiety in the other individual. The dominated individual might feel a depletion of energy, creating a desire to win back energy through a drama play of his or her own. These back-and-forth efforts can then eventually escalate into other "control dramas," which range from passive to aggressive in nature.

Without being conscious of the process, most individuals play out relations in relentless cycles of drama. The following four categories of drama plays are simplifications of roles that are used in a multitude of combinations and degrees. Different circumstances lead to variations in their expression. While there are many types, they are more easily understood when they are explained in their most basic format:

> • *Pity. A dominated individual may develop a sense of victimization. By playing the role of victim, an attempt is made to draw pity from the aggressor and bystanders.*

However, this can be a problematic situation, since this strategy tends to be self-fulfilling – it can encourage more aggression from others.

- ***Distance**. The objective here is to restrict intimate information. Its purpose is to limit facts that might be used for manipulating the targeted individual. The downside is that the possibility of developing mutual understanding is eliminated, since the absence of information creates a type of psychic wall.*
- ***Judgement**. Criticism is used to create self-doubt in the other person. Unfortunately, this pushes the targeted individual into a defensive posture. Furthermore, openness to constructive criticism is destroyed as well, because all forms of criticism become equally suspect.*
- ***Domination**. This is an attempt to forcefully subdue others through intimidation. The downside is that aggression always encourages more*

aggression.

In our childhood, many of us are entangled within cycles of drama. Not being aware that a destructive process is taking place, our young minds are easily saturated with fears and traumas. And as our energy is repeatedly depleted through controlling circumstances, we feel increasingly vulnerable and weakened. Sadly, many abused individuals remain stuck in a victimized state of mind into their adulthood. Other, more resilient individuals are able to develop some immunity and strike back at psychological barriers they have developed. It is only when souls are able to overcome adversarial situations that they grow and move into higher frequencies of expression. Those that are unable to overcome challenges often self-destruct; others join forces of darkness, because that is the only way they know how to strike back.

As children, our options are limited. But as adults, we have the capacity to analyze our experiences logically as well intuitively. Such introspection helps us develop resistance to negative forces, so that we can move forward in fulfilling our potential. Simply being aware of our psychological baggage initiates the healing process – but only if healing is our intention. Unfortunately, some individuals choose to analyze their childhood traumas for less productive reasons; they wish to seek revenge. Thus it is our choice how to react to negative experiences: they can empower us with constructive understanding; or they can embitter us, driving us to the dark side. We choose whether to apply experiences towards our spiritual growth or to denigrate us.

Of course, it is important to acknowledge that social interactions can be quite complicated, due to a variety of circumstances. Our constructive defenses will depend not only on our level of inner strength but also on the type of control dramas we are confronted with. Thus we are challenged to analyze ourselves for personality traits that lead us into difficult situations. Often the Subconscious is crammed with negative behavioral loops; these are core beliefs that contribute to the creation of control dramas to which we are consistently drawn into. We can rise above dysfunctional experiences by being aware of them; this is done through digging deeper within our minds to uncover destructive beliefs. Such introspection can empower us, if we are willing to be 100% honest with ourselves. The process can lead us to healing and balancing of our psyches, so that we are empowered to create constructive expressions in our lives.

Everyone knows that ideal objectives are not necessarily easy to implement. It is no easy task undoing habitual cycles of behavior; nor is replacing them with positive ones instantaneous. For one thing, we never completely succeed in pulling out of control dramas within our own families. Many family members can remain stubbornly ingrained with negative habits, resisting change at any cost. So if dismantling a destructive social scenario proves impossible, we can only take responsibility for our own actions and reactions. We cannot force others to express constructive attitudes – but we can take the high road to other more positive environments.

Since reality requires that we share the world with stubborn personalities, the key is to change ourselves and simply refuse to play by their corrupt games. We do not have to allow others to define the rules; we do not have to accept denigration. We take the upper hand when we insist on working things out on a higher level of expression. Whenever possible, we should step away from destructive games, refusing to exchange energy in the old way. This often forces other players to do some introspection. If they have the initiative, they may come to understand the futility of old habits and adjust to the new, more constructive circumstances. That is the best possible scenario. The worst possibility is that hardcore antagonists will push harder to compensate for the decrease in energy. If the pushing is hard and frequent enough, the drama may continue indefinitely – to the culprit's satisfaction. Or we can simply walk away from the self-destructive scenario. Although not necessarily easy, there is absolutely nothing wrong with walking away from a lose-lose situation. The timing may simply be wrong for absolving the relationship. Or the other participant may be forever lost to dark principles.

The Nature Of Evil. When we choose to take constructive routes, we grow stronger by using our negative experiences for spiritual benefit: We can become more resilient; we can learn empathy for the less fortunate; we can device methods for defeating abusive situations; and we can develop constructive reactions that counteract energy-stealing dramas. These are only some of the many ways that we can turn dark experiences into empowering ones.

Dark forces do not and cannot make us choose debilitation over enlightenment. They can only do what they know – confront us with obstacles and pitfalls in the form of convolutions, contradictions and outright lies. Their hope is that we will eventually stumble and choose their dark philosophy. It is up to us whether to "make lemonade out of lemons" or stoop down to vindictive frequencies. Those who consistently steal energy by abusing others do so because they do not know how to increase their own energy reserves any other way. They are stuck with an attitude based on ignorance, for *evil is the result of being unbalanced in understanding.*

Since Life is a manifestation of yin/yang forces in constant interplay, it is logical that there will be souls who lean towards the dark side of Life. However, when discussing human psychology, the distinction between dark and light forces can be quite complicated.

In regards to humans, evil is not always distinct, since we all incorporate negative as well as positive traits within our psyches. It is certainly unfair to label others as evil simply because we do not agree with their opinions. Nor is it a matter of reserving the term for those who commit criminal acts, because it is possible for anyone to get in trouble with the law to various degrees.

On the other hand, we should not minimize the existence of evil entities – as is popular with some metaphysical groups. Evil obviously exists, since it has clearly manifested itself throughout humanity's history. It also exists beyond our reality in other dimensions. Those who perpetuate the notion that there is no such thing as evil often have the highest intentions, for in the bigger picture, they are quite correct! Everything does have an important role to play within the cycles of Life; evil does play a constructive role in our spiritual evolution.

However, it is equally important to understand the nature of evil at our level of consciousness. In our dimension, evil manifests from a lack of conscience. Individuals who either are born without a conscience or are unable to develop one are incapable of having empathy for others. They are unable to really care what others may feel. Their only interest in others is how they can be used for their own ends. Unfortunately, those without a conscience are not always obviously clear to us, since most of them learn to mimic a conscience. Often pretending to be good Samaritans, they impress society with their good works in the social arena.

People without a conscience can be a tricky lot, because they hide their true nature. Nor do they necessarily appear sinister as we might expect. Stereotypes do not always apply to them. Some of these unbalanced individuals may become heartless criminals, but most of them become "respectable" leaders of major institutions. They can be respected CEOs of international corporations, heads of prominent families, national leaders or even religious superiors. Many find their "true calling" as religious leaders because it is easy for them to manipulate others in the name of faith. They are able to perform in a variety of leading roles by developing excellent acting skills, something they learn as a survival technique.

Lacking a true conscience, they are not bothered by moral restrictions. Nor do they feel any guilt in manipulating those who do have a conscience. Another characteristic of sociopaths is that some of them are unable to feel emotion, so that they are encapable of expressing their hatred. Thus they are not necessarily hateful by nature. Of course, this seems ironic. They do, however, manifest disdain towards humanity. They especially find "do-gooders" intolerable and often target them, attempting to bring them down.

Being especially dependent on their egos for guidance, they find a sense of security by controlling everyone in their lives. One way they do this is by spreading fear, doubt and confusion, whenever and wherever the opportunity arises. Simply put, they desire to extinguish truth and "light," which they find annoying and contrary to their view of Life. And because they tend to have a persuasive nature, they can easily confuse unsuspecting victims, thereby drawing them into their sphere of influence.

Nevertheless, while it is important to understand the true nature of evil, it is equally important to not obsess over it, because it can have destructive repercussions in our lives. This happens in two ways: it distracts us from other important issues, while gradually corrupting our sense of equilibrium. While acknowledging that evil exists, we must simultaneously focus on the polarized nature of reality. That is, we must focus on the ***wholeness*** of

Life, that everything has both negative and positive qualities. It is a matter of developing a balance between knowing and obsessing. The ideal is to become aware of the role negativity plays in Life without being drawn into its destructive compulsion. Personal introspection must be a matter of emphasizing the positive aspects of Life, while understanding the workings of yin/yang forces in the universe.

Life In Degrees, Angles & Polarities. Since Life is about change, nothing can exist in a static state; nothing can remain permanently in stillness. Everything in the universe is perpetually in the process of either: (1) growing, (2) changing or (3) disintegrating. Unfortunately, some individuals choose to express the dynamic of perpetual change through negative mode, which is certainly a tragic way to live. But from their perspective, they are fulfilling their destiny, for they sense that their purpose is to shake things up from the yin side of Life. Of course, embracing the dark side means being led towards ever deeper expressions of negativity.

There are also individuals who are not willing to choose sides. They attempt to remain neutral in that they stay away from the dark as well as the light side of reality. But maintaining such an expressionless, neutral attitude is impossible to keep forever. Eventually, they are forced to pick a side, because refusing to nurture a positive attitude eventually defaults to dark expressions. This is because the universe is incapable of remaining static – it must grow in consciousness or move in the other direction as negativity. There is no such thing as a static existence! The choice is quite simple: Either we grow, or we are drawn to negativity.

If we wish to reach our full potential, we have to find equilibrium in our lives. This requires understanding the negativity in our lives, which is a matter of always remembering three premises:
- *Life moves with the principle of yin/yang;*
- *Everything manifests in degrees and angles, while constantly striving for balance;*
- *Turning away from evil is not a weakness. It is simply refusing to play by its rules.*

The Triad. If Life is polarized by nature, how can we use this principle to initiate and maintain higher consciousness? Since control dramas are not the answer, we must find another way to exchange energy with others. Life does offer an alternative: We can develop a holistic perspective. This is not a matter of eliminating negativity or the ego from our lives but of *integrating* polarities into a greater third force. This is the Triad, which finds expression as an uplifting spiral of energy. It is referred to as Triadic because it is essentially a triad of three forces: yin, yang and the blending of the two. As the perfect balancing of polarities, it is symbolized by the Tao symbol. This emblem is a combination of yin and yang representations, which together create the third aspect – its wholeness.

Attuning to the Triadic Essence means resisting emotional baits and avoiding destructive entanglements whenever possible. By focusing on the concept of equilibrium, we shift gears into the Third Force. Not only can we learn to not force things through our egos, but we can also learn to recognize meaningful insights. These are important messages from our Higher Selves. It is simply a matter of keeping our minds open to new information and opportunities. In the process, frequencies of peace and harmony can increase in our lives, so that we are lifted into a higher plane of consciousness. As we learn to surf the turbulent waves of Life, we also come to understand how everything fits within the bigger picture – within the greater scheme of things. As we learn to attune ourselves to the Triadic Force, we move beyond an arena of polarization into a higher consciousness where we are freed of constrictive attitudes and dark thoughts. We become freer to experiment with the choices and wonders that the universe offers us.

100

101

CHAPTER FIVE

GRACE IS YOUR STRENGTH

Deep inside each of us pulses the desire to be one with the universe, echoing the question "What is my connection to Life?" The answer is *a universal frequency that shines with the brilliance of all reality.* This dynamic principle is divine grace. It is the most eloquent of all forces, for it supports and holds all things together.

It is a fact that humans need the love of others to not only survive but to thrive as well. For instance, orphanages throughout the world have learned that babies must be picked up, rocked and touched on a regular basis. Otherwise, they develop severe emotional handicaps, or they fail to survive at all. Thus there is no doubt that love is essential for human development.

An interesting aspect of love is that we can love others without liking them. For example, there is the religious angle of "loving the sinner but not the sin." However, this is simply an attempt to promote *conditional* love by separating the sinner from the sin. This approach would never work with grace, because – by its very virtue – the true magnificence of grace never lends itself to such corruption. Divine grace can *never* be diminished into "conditional grace." No such thing can be! *Divine grace always refers to unconditional acceptance – and much more!*

Because it has the finest essence imaginable, grace has not been detected by scientific means. However, Quantum Physics will eventually reveal it as an algorithmic equation. Even now, physicists continue their search for the *Theory of Everything* – a mathematical equation that ties all realities into one simple expression.

Quantum Mechanics describes how very small particles like electrons and atoms – and even smaller ones – behave in ways contrary to conventional expectations. In order to understand Quantum Mechanics, we have to divorce ourselves from everyday reality; we have to accept that we live in a porous, dream-like universe. In deeper reality, solids are more like gases, and gases are more like empty space. This is why mystics are interested in Quantum Physics – because it offers evidence that there is more to the world than what our eyes perceive.

The Dynamics of Connection. We live in a universe organized by natural laws of physics and biology. What initiates and moves these universal laws is a field referred to as *"the Matrix,"* a type of inter-dimensional canvas with interlocking webs that connect all things. And in fact, the very *fabric* of the universe is imprinted within this hyper-space. It sustains and inter-connects all of reality, maintaining it in a vibrant state of existence. Without the Matrix nothing would ever exist, for it is the core and initiator of anything and everything that *becomes*.

Humanity's potential is as great as sages have taught for millennia, for our very thoughts affect the universe in a manner never imagined before. It is important to our role as co-creators that we understand the power that we exercise through the Matrix: *it responds to our emotional energy, without reservation.* Thus our ability to move the universe through the Matrix carries a heavy responsibility. We have to control our attitudes and beliefs, for they affect Life more than we ever realized. If we simply observe the world, we can see the powerful effect that our emotions have on other people as well as on all living things. It is a fact that plants, animals and people sense and respond to our emotional energy. Thus living our lives by a philosophy based on this understanding – of our cosmic connections – is not only the ideal; it is the most practical and constructive.

Unfortunately, many of us have been taught by contemporary society that we must repress our feelings. But this belief is obviously based on ignorance. For one thing, repressing feelings only blocks them temporarily – their energy does not dissipate. Initially, repressed feelings may remain obstructed but they eventually explode at unexpected moments. If their metaphysical implications hold true, then society should be instructing us on how to *control* them, rather than repressing them. Directing our emotions in constructive, creative directions is the real solution.

At another level, because they are fearful of others, some individuals coarsen their attitudes. They do not hesitate to brutalize others in the name of survival. But this is a demonstration of ignorance, for negative emotion cut both ways: they are double-edged swords that hurt us as much as they hurt others.

We must accept that, not only are feelings perfectly natural, but to express them is to express our power. Of course, the goal must be to exercise them in a responsible manner. That is, emotion must not control us; we must learn to control our emotional energy. It should be obvious that what makes us special is our ability to exercise this awesome energy with *intent*, because emotion is the mover of reality.

We live in a responsive, dynamic world in which intentions radiate throughout the Matrix, ultimately affecting everything they touch. No other life-form approximates this ability.

Lessons Of Discord. Our emotional connection is important in a variety of ways. For example, the emotional fields of individuals merge in what is referred to as *"emotional co-dependence."* Such mingling of energies is usually positive. But there can be a downside. When relationships disintegrate into power struggles, the result is the creation of destructive thought forms. When we "keep score" in our relationships, we are simply giving life to a destructive form. Often, we gradually begin to notice more the mistakes that others make, and less and less appreciating their worthiness. As the "score cards" add up, resentment gradually decreases the exchange of positive energy. Instead, the increase of negativity empowers a dividing form between the two, until the relationship collapses. Then a control drama develops, because it is the only energy that will sustain the relationship, even if it is a dysfunctional one.

Control dramas are simply a corrupt attempt to regain the energy exchange that diminishes from lack of love. Individuals clash, as they seek common factors in their relationship. In lieu of mutual respect, criticism becomes the lowest common denominator in a failing relationship.

Often, the fear of being alone motivates individuals to accept a dysfunctional relationship as a substitute for true love. This sad scenario implies that both individuals are trapped in an endless power struggle. While one individual may periodically profess love for the other, yet he or she may actually be attempting to manipulate the relationship. Wherever possible, the domineering one attempts to make the controlling decisions.

And while some desire to control others in the name of love, submissive individuals may seek out aggressive personalities for complementary reasons. Thus there are no innocent victims in dysfunctional relationships. The resulting situation is an arena of emotional give and take based on disdain rather than mutual respect. Eventually, this type of relationship leads to self-destruction for both individuals, because it is an unbalanced equation that cannot be sustained indefinitely.

A balanced relationship is one in which *no one puts limitations on love, for it means limiting Life.* When people love each other in the highest possible sense, they share their lives of their own choice. And their love is greater because of that freedom.

Above all, the most challenging lesson is that of self forgiveness. We must always forgive ourselves for being less than ideal, for not understanding challenging experiences. We must give ourselves permission to possibly fall into entrapments of negativity, because no one can realistically go through Life without ever making mistakes.

If we become critical of ourselves, we become critical of others as well; this can then lead to hatred.

And of course, sometimes we deceive ourselves into believing that we are justified in hating others. This is because hatred is always self-justifying. *The individual who feels hatred prejudges the nature of reality and always finds excuses to hate.* Once he or she decides to hate, no rationale changes their mind.

People who see mostly ugliness in their lives have mostly themselves to blame. If negativity is all they notice, it is because that is their preoccupation; they are centered in negativity. However, hatred is a lose-lose situation, a dead-end zone for anyone caught in its obsession.

The Dynamics Of Grace. The "good news" is that there is a better way to cope with Life. We don't have to settle for contentious relationships. Nor do we have to submit to self-loathing. The power of grace empowers us to move beyond egotistical inclinations of judgement. It leads us into deeper and wider levels of understanding, were we can learn to live according to higher qualities. Grace is the key to a higher standard of living – it empowers us to fulfill our potential as co-creators.

Undoubtedly, learning about grace can be difficult for many individuals, because many are marred with convoluted ideas that demean and weaken humanity. Although no one suddenly snaps into the virtue of grace, we can inch towards it every day, in every way. Simply making an effort to understand the dynamics of grace guarantees that we at least move in the right direction, for intent means everything in the Game of Life.

The simplest definition of grace refers to *"the principle of unconditional goodwill."* Always, the ethic is to give and receive energy – never to forcefully take it. It means respecting others unconditionally, without keeping score cards and never judging their worth in the greater scope of Life. It means allowing others the right to be themselves, while we focus on their best qualities.

In contentious situations, the message should always be: "You are a good person, but your *actions* have caused me pain." It should never be a struggle of egos, for such struggles are without end. Rather, living with the virtue of grace means learning to terminate cycles of drama or walking away from them, for there is no shame or weakness in this.

Regardless of the dramas we encounter, we can take ownership of them, because taking responsibility for all our experiences is the first step towards virtuous living. It should be understood that the Game of Life always includes challenging situations. As long as there are lessons to be learned, Life will continue to draw us into learning experiences. We will continue to encounter individuals with complementary needs, for that is the cycle of Life. As we experience various situations, we should remember that the other participants need something from us – whether a lesson, inspiration or simply a shake-up. Likewise, we probably need something from them as well! This is the Synchronicity Principle: *Accepting that all individuals come into our lives for a greater good is a super win-win situation for everyone.*

These exchanges can be positive or negative, depending on our level of understanding. We do have choices. We can integrate the power of grace into our lives, so that experiences become more like surfing the waves of Life. Or we can continue being confrontational, so that it feels like we are fighting one battle after another in an endless war.

Behind all power struggles, there is a spiritual lesson about the dynamics of love. Since Life teaches through interpersonal experiences, the first lesson is to uplift others whenever possible. Merely surviving on a day-to-day basis is not really living; such an existence lacks spiritual depth and endeavor. It is only when we are able to move beyond the "walking dead" stage that we live our potential as co-creators.

As we struggle to find our happiness, we must refrain from judging others. A judgmental attitude would imply disrespect for the adventures that others have embarked on. We are all here for the same purpose: to find our perfection. And as we cannot blame a child for not being an adult, likewise we must gracefully appreciate the "mistakes" of humanity. We must uplift whenever and however we can, for that is where humanity's hope lies. When we uplift rather than hinder, we uplift ourselves as well, for a society is as strong as its weakest link!

However, many individuals misinterpret spiritual insights. Striving for spiritual enlightenment does not require demeaning oneself. It does not mean we should be stupid or lacking in self-respect. Most certainly, practicing the art of grace does *not* mean exposing ourselves to abuse. Rather, it is about cutting through cycles of drama, releasing score cards and developing inner peace. Grace is about understanding that abusers do their best according to their level of awareness. Without judgment, we must always strive to comprehend the circumstances and intentions held by others. However, simultaneously, we must give ourselves permission to steer away from dark experiences initiated by others. We are not required to participate in experiences that we find unacceptable; we are only required to learn how to respond in a graceful manner.

116

The most beautiful thing that we can do is imprint graciousness in all our experiences. Primarily, this is a matter of continually re-affirming a sense of respect in every situation, while even allowing ourselves the possibility of failure with this endeavor. Ultimately, our frailties are expressed for that sole purpose: to challenge us to accept ourselves unconditionally. Mistakes are allowed so that they may eventually pave our path to a sense of perfection, a state where we come to understand that everyone is worthy of a life blessed with graciousness.

117

DYNAMICS

CHAPTER SIX

PICTURE IT PERFECT

The power of imagination is greater than most people appreciate. It echoes beyond the known physical world, moving through countless dimensions, then reflecting back to us. Because of its limitless potential, imagination is the greatest mental faculty that we possess. While the masses are now awakening to this revelation, it is an insight that has been well understood by sages for millennia.

That there are other dimensional realities is now an established premise within the field of Quantum Physics. The *Matrix Theory* proposes a unified view of reality, stating that our three-dimensional universe is contained within a much larger multi-dimensional hyper-space. This area – also referred to as a cosmic canvas, or super-space – contains all of reality, all dimensions, all worlds and all universes.

The Nature Of Reality. The famous equation of $E=MC_2$ (Energy = Mass x Speed of Light, squared) states that energy and matter are interchangeable, that all things are simply variations of electro-magnetic (EM) charges. Different EM frequencies establish the variations that manifest within each dimensional reality. More specifically, three factors affect the nature of every dimensional realm: (1) superstrings, (2) atomic elements, and (3) subatomic bonding. In the future, we will understand how these factors interrelate to each other in a deeper fashion. For now, we assume that they are different factors within each dimension:

• *Superstrings.* Just as a violin string can be made to vibrate in multiple modes, so do the fundamental quantum strings vibrate within each dimension. These "strings" move at different frequencies, according to their dimensional qualities. Of course, these cosmic superstrings are far different from violin strings. For one thing, they are composed of electro-magnetic energy, and they manifest beyond the simple dimensional space of up-down, left-right, and forward-backward, which we find in our own three-dimensional (3D) realm.

For instance, in some of the "higher" dimensions, the singularity of time is replaced by a unified space-time field, where it is expressed without a linear effect. To get a general idea of how space-time manifests uniquely in our own reality as a linear expression, consider our linear movements through our 3D universe: As we proceed through time, we carve out a "tube" that manifests within hyper-space. And at each point in time, we are faced by many optional futures to choose from. In a reality without linear time, sequences of events would not be perceived in a linear fashion but in a circular one!

• *Atomic Elements.* As far as our 3D world goes, quarks and leptons are the smallest units of quasi-matter. In turn, these fundamental particle-waves make up the atom, which can be compared to a mini solar system – with the electrons orbiting the nucleus – except that gravity plays no role. Instead, an electro-magnetic force holds the electrons near the nucleus. The number and type of protons and neutrons in its center determines the manifested substance.

• *Subatomic Bonding.* The frequency of a particular substance is also dictated by the distance of nucleus to electron. Because it is difficult to comprehend the quasi-material nature of atoms, then consider this analogy: If the nucleus of an atom is compared to the size of a grain of salt, the electrons rotating around it would be hundreds of feet away from it. Now, with this in mind, think about the wide space between the nucleus and electrons. The distance of electrons from the nucleus is called the shell, but in actuality it is simply energy. And the larger the shell distance, the more energy is required to maintain the electrons in orbit. So, in "higher" dimensions, wider atomic shells are maintained by greater energy levels.

The Creative Principle. When our thoughts are intense, they often manifest quickly after incubating in hyper-space. The process is a somewhat complex evolutionary phenomenon. But essentially, ideas are energized, amplified and then projected back into our 3D reality as actual events. Just as material matter is a form of energy, so are events a *matrix* of billions of energy patterns interacting, commingling and intertwining with each other. In fact, Life is a vast sequence of energy patterns, constantly shifting in a sea of probabilities. Each universe is essentially a conglomeration of manifested thought-forms! And just as electricity is magnetism in motion, *thought is mind in action.* Thought consciousness is a real, active force that exerts itself upon the universe. That is, consciousness is not merely passive awareness – it is also a tangible force that affects other energy fields as well as physical objects. It affects everything!

In our 3D reality, we live with the illusion that Life is a sequence of accidental events, each set in concrete terms. But in fact, Life begins in the mind –

in our conscious thinking – and then manifests in the world as experience. *We live through a chain of thought manifestations.*

Absolutely nothing happens by chance; we live in a perfect universe moved by cosmic principles. Every effect has its cause; every occurrence happens because there are forces which propel it into existence. We are witnesses to a universe based on a system of law and order. Every day, we are able to depend on the predictability of natural forces that direct gravity, rotation of the Earth, rain, sunshine and many other phenomenal occurrences. From the subatomic level to complex life-forms, everything is under creative guidance. Every *thing* and every *event* happens because it was conceived somewhere.

Thus it should become clear that our presence on Earth resonates throughout the universe, because our consciousness is of high intensity. Actuality, more than that, it resonates throughout the multi-dimensional hyper-universe! Our strong thought projections are unique to humankind, for no other life-form matches our ability to manipulate consciousness to the degree that we do. Without our direct participation, natural forces constantly push and pull – in endless ways – to materialize the thoughts we endow with willpower. Our power of thought guarantees that each of us, no matter who we are, takes part in the creative process of Life; we are co-creators of the universe.

Needless to say, many of humanity's thoughts are of a negative, destructive or corrupted quality. Because we all manipulate reality, whether or not we are aware of the process, it is imperative that we learn to exercise our consciousness in the most balanced manner possible. Otherwise, many of our experiences will continue to be of a destructive nature. We bring into our lives those persons, things, circumstances, conditions and happenings which we desire, accept or fear. Thus our ability to move reality brings great responsibility.

Elements Of Resonance. Simply by the *beliefs* we embrace, we choose how to move reality.

When we believe in specific things or circumstances, we give them life; we sustain and reinforce them. Too many individuals refuse to accept this immense responsibility. They even revolt at the mere suggestion that their consciousness resonates at the center of their reality; they prefer to leave all responsibility with a universal creator. But with the power of "freedom of choice" comes consequences: We are required to learn how to exercise our freedom with equilibrium.

However, accepting our mental capabilities can be the beginning to even greater expressions of power. Knowing about it is only the first step towards transforming our lives. If our very thoughts produce tangible effects when used unconsciously, imagine the powerful effects when they are applied in a *purposeful* manner. The results can appear amazingly magical at times.

If we wish to control our fate, then we must also be willing to take responsibility for our creative abilities. This is regardless of whether we speak of our intellectual or metaphysical capabilities; all our mental powers have consequences. Although we are challenged with many limitations – such as conflicts, convoluted beliefs and fears – we are also endowed with the power to overcome them. We have the mental, emotional and spiritual resources to construct our future reality as we see fit. The basic requirements are that we: (1) accept our abilities, (2) exercise them and (3) project them in the most balanced manner possible. We have the power to control and fashion our fate to something approximating the ideal. Only, we need to have the faith to initiate and sustain the process.

With this understanding, there is no reason for anyone to feel trapped by the drama of Life. If we create and re-create our lives by our own thoughts, then we can change the quality of our thoughts and thereby the quality of our experiences. But we alone can express our consciousness. Having the power to choose how to think is both our power and as well as our responsibility; it is our unique talent as *artists of reality*.

At the deepest and highest reality, there are three fundamental creative elements which regulate thought manifestation: (1) intent, (2) imagination and (3) conviction:

• *Intent.* The primary element of mental creation is defined as the "focusing and directing of an idea." Intent can also be defined as the combination of *desire and willpower.* We usually project our intentions without giving them too much energy or contemplation. This is our natural inclination, since we take the process for granted on a daily basis. Without strong willpower or feeling, most of our intended ideas usually simply fizzle out. However, when we focus them with discipline and real desire, their power is intensified and thereby amplified. The greater the focus or willpower, the stronger becomes the *coherence* of a thought-form. Feelings – also expressed as desire – are what become the *core* of our intents. And it is around this core to which electro-magnetic energies coalesce, eventually causing them to manifest in our three-dimensional world. Thus strength of structure as well as desire dictate a thought-form's ability to find expression in our reality. Of course, manifestation can take any number of shapes, depending on the nature of the thought. It can be an event, situation or material object – anything, really.

• *Imagination.* The second element in mental creation is imagery. Whereas intent is the spark which ignites an idea, imagery creates the framework around which the thought-out event, circumstance or thing is formed. As a skill, the use of imagination can involve verbal assertion as well as physical action, if it assists us. While holding imagined scenarios in our minds, we can rely on the repetition of a phrase or word (mantras). This is a matter of using a pattern of steady, deliberate repetitive words. Or we can beat a drum as well as. Any action that helps us remain focused on the target image for more than a few seconds aids our ability to sustain the image. Chanting and drumming not only helps us remain in a focused mode, they also block out distractions like nearby noises and movements. The focused image is then able to continually draw more energy to itself, until it manifests in our 3D reality.

Rhythm by means of mantras or drumming is the most common means by which skilled meditators focus their imagery. But mantras have more power than merely sustaining focus: they can have a real, physical impact, if they are of the right pitch and frequency. Just as a musical note can shatter glass, rhythmic patterned words can create energetic structures. Besides sound, rhythm can occur as patterns of motion, light or any other factor. Rhythmic motion is a normal thing and is very much a part of Life. In fact, Nature itself manifests as rhythmic cycles.

• *Conviction*. Active belief is the third important element of mental creation. It can be the most challenging aspect, since a leap of faith is required at times. When we reject ideas, we push them away, even destroying them at times. If we view things or concepts with disbelief, we crush their power, even if that is not our intention. On the other hand, by expecting our dreams to come true, we take ownership of them. Nothing in Life is accomplished without having faith to some degree. We can empower ideas simply by believing in them – this imbues them with the spark of resolve.

Our projected conviction can be enhanced by verbalizing our intentions. By actually stating aloud our objectives, we enhance their validation within our minds. This is a common principle behind all forms of meditation, including prayer.

Opportunity Meets Preparation. The power of luck is simply being prepared to recognize and take opportunities as they present themselves. While it is important to deliberately envision success, it is just as important to actively participate in its manifestation. Regardless of whether we believe in the principles of creation, Life continues with or without our active part. Therefore, we can choose to simply be spectators. Or we can choose to be active participants, coloring the world with our own inspirations. In melodic form, *we can create our own wings of destiny by entwining hope with action.*

132

133

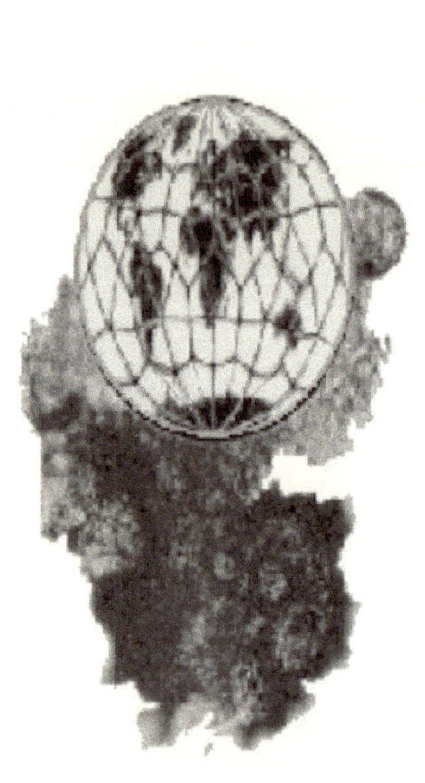

REFLECTIONS

CHAPTER SEVEN

THE WORLD IS YOUR MIRROR

Interconnecting global awareness into a unified consciousness is as important as unifying our own psyches. As we concern ourselves with our inner consciousness, our understanding of the bigger picture will expand as a result. This will naturally motivate many of us to reach out to the world, because the two are really reflections of each another. Thus, as our creative abilities increase, they will reflect with greater frequency in the global arena – our hopes, dreams and values will manifest with greater force.

As we learn to unify and defragmentize our divided consciousness, we will be projecting the same healing process into the social environment. As we heal, so will the world. And as we reinforce our sense of self-worth, we will project this same worthiness outwards into the global arena. In this manner, our inner healing will regenerate the world simultaneously, for the connection between it and us is a very real one. If there has been a sense of separation, it is because the ego has harbored that elusion. As more individuals wake up and see the bigger picture, they will be expressing more of their Higher Selves and less of their egotistical carelessness. As the number of awakened souls reaches a critical mass, global consciousness will resonate with their positive force. In fact, the unfolding of this higher consciousness will resonate beyond our planet and into endless dimensions, because there is no limit to our creative expression. Thus, we are reminded of the importance of becoming attuned with our Higher Selves.

Sacred Geometry. As we increase our awareness of the greater reality, we will be looking deeper into the depths of Life, where we will find amazing geometrical beauty throughout the universe. Those who will be most surprised will be researchers inclined to think purely in logical terms. Humanity will finally understand – really know – that there is a real *intelligence* behind and within all things. Those who believe that Life is the result of innumerable mistakes will be hard pressed to explain the orderliness inherent in all forms. Whether alive or otherwise, from atoms to galaxies, we find meaningful shapes and forms that are impossible to replicate through chaotic means.

The orderliness that we will find universally throughout reality is the subject of *Sacred Geometry*. Essentially, it is the study and interpretation of the mathematical aspects of all things in Life. In fact, this field of study expounds mathematics as the language of divine creation; it is asserted that it is also the means for organizing everything. For this reason, the studying of Sacred Geometry expands our view of reality; it does so by unifying our logical and intuitive minds within a higher consciousness. When we integrate our polarized hemispheres in this manner, we enhance our understanding of Life. In this manner our ability to perceive the deeper reality of things is expanded as well.

Gaia Consciousness. An important concept resulting from Sacred Geometry is the *Gaia Matrix*. This is the name given to the Earth's planetary eco-system. The term "Gaia" describes the totality of Life on the planet – this includes everything affecting living systems, such as the atmosphere, soil, forests, deserts and all other living environments. Historically, Gaia was the ancient Greek name for the goddess known as "Earth." The "Matrix" refers to a natural global network of energy; some of this energy follows in straight lines; some flows according to natural geographical structures; and sometimes it finds expression as points or whirls. Just as the human body contains a matrix of energy points, so does our planet radiate her own centers of power – vortices. Thus the planetary Matrix is an energy web linking the globe together. It includes a total of twelve major vortices, six of which reside on each side of the equator.

The Gaia Matrix is therefore the wholeness of life-forms, environments and energy patterns found on the Earth. All of these are known to be affected by many factors. These influences include – but are not limited to – electro-magnetic fields, sun storms, cosmic rays and even our own thoughts!

Ancient cultures from both East and West recognized that energy moved through the Earth. But they came to slightly different conclusions; therefore, they studied the energy flows from two distinct perspectives. In the East, the energy patterns were described as "dragon currents," which were said to follow the natural landscape. The West, in contrast, focused on "ley lines," which are straight geometric connections between vortex points. From these two viewpoints in Eastern and Western cultures came *"Feng Shui"* and *"Geomancy,"* respectively. Although their conclusions are often identical, their interpretations can also be complementary. Thus the difference between the two is simply a matter of geometric focus; that is, it is a matter of what details they chose to concentrate on. In reality, both studies do not contradict but supplement each other; both perspectives are equally valid.

Feng Shui (translated as "Wind-Water")

essentially studies the harmonious flow of chi (life force) within environments – such as the home, work place or any other area of human commune. Geomancy, on the other hand, focused on finding the intersection of straight ley lines. This is where temples and churches were often established. In both Eastern and Western cultures, energy experts advised on the proper placement of buildings, insuring that they were bathed with harmonious energy.

Partially based on the ancient studies of Feng Shui as well as Geomancy, *Gaiagraphy* was developed as a modern "science of the living Earth." But it is more than simply an integration of the two older studies. Gaiagraphy is essentially an integrative science of geometry, geography and sociology – but from an energy point of view. It attempts to modernize ancient techniques of identifying and directing Earth energies by applying modern scientific principles. Geometrical structures, geographical topography and electro-magnetic lines are some of the factors given consideration within Gaiagraphic studies of homes and settlements. More than than simply analyzing physical structure, Gaiagraphy identifies the energetic essence of a home or community as well.

As a study of our living planet and places of commune, the new science looks at the human species as part of symbiotic systems within a larger planetary one. Its greatest utility is at the communal level, i.e. town and city planning. While individual living places are studied, the relationship of individuals to the community is also important. Furthermore, the micro (smallest) as well as the macro (largest) elements are looked at within the bigger perspective. In other words, the tiniest energy structure is analyzed for its effects on the largest energy structure, and vice versa.

Global Consciousness. While we rarely think about it, modern civilization is actually the result of *"mass thinking."* What is different from the past is that, instead of "imposed thinking" from a dominant class or leader, mainstream citizens are emerging as the dominant force propelling mass ideas. Of course, it is a matter of degree, since "Big Brother" is always at work attempting manipulation and control of the masses. Nevertheless, the new humanity will be composed of reflective, creative thinkers, with an expanding sense of grace. Expanding our hearts will be important, because hatred is the number one obstacle to spiritual development; it blurs our vision and warps our discernment.

Two phenomena are propelling the creation of a new *cosmopolitan paradigm*: (1) thought contagion and (2) world wide communications – especially "the Internet." Although the new consciousness has been building up through eons of time, only recently has it begun reaching *critical mass*. This refers to a point, level or strength at which major changes are initiated and sustained; it results in a chain reaction of new, unfolding circumstances.

Thought Contagion. At a psychological level, this term refers to the development of telepathic rapport among humanity, but it is really much more. Since every individual's consciousness is connected with the larger mass consciousness –the *Collective*

Unconscious – all thoughts and experiences are accessible to everyone; this is because everyone's consciousness is actually integrated in a larger communal reality. The phrase, "the one is part of the whole, and the whole is composed of each one," rings true, because thought contagion is based on psychological as well as psychic realities.

Because we are all interconnected in this Collective Unconscious, the power of our thoughts can be compounded within this mental arena. In this mental environment there is the possibility of psychological as well as psychic amplification. Not only do our thoughts resonate at an energetic level, but ideas can create chain reactions that reverberate with a snow-balling effect. When individual minds integrate with the mass consciousness, certain concepts can eventually accumulate strength – this is thought contagion in its simplest form.

The Internet. The networking of computer systems around the globe has been compared to an externalization of our Collective Unconscious.

Theoretically, the Internet can enhance thought contagion by helping to spread information more rapidly. It will insure that individual thoughts have instantaneous impact on global consciousness. Our new sense of universal community will eventually transform old, stagnant paradigms into new cosmopolitan expressions. The Internet will prove to be a powerful means for exploding rigid psychologies and developing a new creative realm for constructive expression. Already, the masses in some nations have relied on this technological marvel to instigate and coordinate democratic revolutions.

New Frontiers. Understanding our strengths implies an unspoken responsibility. It should be clear that each and every individual makes a real difference in the global community. Each of us can choose to uplift or degrade the world according to our personal expressions. In other words, we must become aware of our ability to enhance harmony or promote discord. As we develop a deeper understanding of Life, learning to work in a spirit of brotherhood will no longer be an empty rhyme.

Today, our thoughts already resonate with ever greater force, whether we are conscious of the process or not. Our thoughts are blending, fusing and intertwining into powerful thought-forms that are coalescing into global events. As our personal thoughts naturally connect with other thoughts, reinforcing and strengthening their common focus, they are affecting other individuals; and those individuals are affecting yet others. The effect is a rippling of ever greater circles of influence. Ordinary individuals are no longer so ordinary! Multiplied by the billions throughout the world, the masses are having a greater impact than they suspect.

It is our challenge to become cognizant of our personal power, taking time to focus an optimistic vision for the world. Spending a few moments each day blessing the world is important because the hellish conditions that have manifested on Earth have been reflections of our own fears. Not only have we witnessed these hells, but we have actually *created* them! Reality has been a reflection of our inner horrors.

Thus we must become equally aware of our ability to create idyllic realities. A new, progressive world *will* manifest as we claim our power as co-creators. Nevertheless, it is important to realize that global conditions will worsen before they get better. This is because our amplified consciousness will first lead to a clearing of repressed negativity before eventually leading to positive expression. The evil that many will see will appear as if we were being punished for our sinfulness or karma. But Life does not rationalize anything as "goodness" or "badness" – that is humanity's realm. Rather, the collective whole of humanity will be releasing fears and judgments that have been repressed for eons of time.

We mustn't allow fear to continue dictating our reality. We can choose to either coarsen our hearts or to open them further to new possibilities. If we choose to courageously face forthcoming events, we will inevitably rise above them. We will collectively resolve new challenges with new impetus. For instance, the principle of *conflict resolution* will become a practical alternative to violence. Even now, the process is gaining ground among companies, organizations, institutions and even nations. Eventually, rather than relying on war, it will be the normal procedure for handling conflicts.

If we are to fulfill our role as custodians of the Earth, we must be willing to take a leap of faith. As we shift our reality into a higher frequency, we will simply *know* how to resolve many "unsolvable" problems. Solutions will become apparent when none seemed possible before. This is because we will be looking at reality with a wider sense of awareness.

Although Earth is beautiful in its own right – in a natural, raw fashion – it is humanity that will bestow her with a higher frequency that she would otherwise not experience. Our planet would never be as magnificent without the enhanced consciousness that a transformed humanity will impress upon it. As we advance as a species, the imbalances that we presently perceive throughout the world will eventually be replaced with divine reflection. Equilibrium will gradually unfold in the world, as more individuals refuse to be slaves to a destructive destiny. Rather, we will be learning to be masters of our own future. Just as humanity learned to "crawl" out of its primitive state, it is now learning to "walk" into progressive awareness, and eventually it will be "flying" into the endless horizon of divine consciousness.

As humanity gradually shifts its reality into higher gear, we will be experiencing wondrous, miraculous events. In a symbiotic partnership with Mother Gaia, we will rise above the old horrors of savagery into new expressions of power. Most certainly, gracious virtue will be a reflection of the new reality, because it will be our salvation. As critical mass reaches the point of no return, we will shift into this grand dream – a vision of idealism that only a few once believed possible.

150

BIBLIOGRAPHY
& RECOMMEND READING

Alder, Vera Stanley. *The Finding of the Third Eye*. 1960.
Arntz, William. *What the Bleep do We Know?* 2005.
Besant, Annie & C.W. Leadbeater. *Thought-Forms*. 1925.
Buscalia, Leo. *Love - A Warm and Wonderful Book About the Largest Experience in Life*. 1972.
Capra, Fritjof. *The Tao of Physics*. 1975.
Hans, Jenny. *"Visualizing Sound." Science Journal*. June 1968.
Hilarion. *Dark Robes. Dark Brothers*. 1981.
Keyes, Ken. *Handbook to Higher Consciousness*. 1975.
Kryon (Lee Carroll). *Books, Volumes I to X*. 1993-2004.
NcGill, Ormond. *Hypnotism & Mysticism of India*. 1979.
Ramtha (JZ Knight). *The Mystery of Love*. 1996.
Redfield, James. *The Celestine Prophecy*. 1993.
Roberts, Jane. *The Nature of Personal Reality*. 1974.
School for Esoteric Studies. *Building and Bridging*. Asheville, NC.
Sheldrake, Rupert. *A New Science of Life*. 1981.
Watson, Lyall. *Supernature*. 1973.

www.ingramcontent.com/pod-product-compliance
Lightning Source LLC
Chambersburg PA
CBHW032124090426
42743CB00007B/449